CLAY TESTING

CLAY TESTING

The clay/non-clay ratio measurement technique
for ceramic stoves

Dr Anura Gaspe, Dr Peter Messer and Pete Young

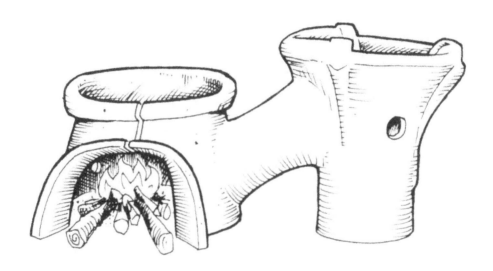

PRACTICAL ACTION
Publishing

Practical Action Publishing Ltd
27a Albert Street, Rugby, CV21 2SG, Warwickshire, UK
www.practicalactionpublishing.org

© Intermediate Technology Publications 1994

First published 1994\Digitised 2008

ISBN 10: 1 85339 266 9
ISBN 13: 9781853392665
ISBN Library Ebook: 9781780443980
Book DOI: http://dx.doi.org/10.3362/9781780443980

A catalogue record for this book is available from the British Library.

The authors, contributors and/or editors have asserted their rights under
the Copyright Designs and Patents Act 1988 to be identified as authors of
their respective contributions.

Since 1974, Practical Action Publishing has published and disseminated
books and information in support of international development work
throughout the world. Practical Action Publishing is a trading name
of Practical Action Publishing Ltd (Company Reg. No. 1159018), the
wholly owned publishing company of Practical Action. Practical Action
Publishing trades only in support of its parent charity objectives and any
profits are covenanted back to Practical Action (Charity Reg. No. 247257,
Group VAT Registration No. 880 9924 76).

Contents

Acknowledgements

This book is the result of four years of clay research and testing at the School of Materials, Sheffield University. It has involved a large number of organizations around the world and we would like to thank them all for their support and co-operation.

We would like to accord a special acknowledge to Toby Harrison who gave us much support at the outset and throughout the project. Sadly, Toby died in 1992.

We would also like to thank Tim Jones and Auke Koopman. Both are experienced ceramists who have provided valuable knowledge and direction to this project.

Finally we thank the Overseas Development Administration of the UK Government for funding this project and enabling Dr Anura Gaspe to gain his Ph.D., and DGIS of the Netherlands for funding an international meeting to discuss the results of this work.

1. Introduction

The main purpose of this manual is to give guidance on the selection and, when necessary, the modification of natural or raw clays from which durable pottery stoves and stove liners can be fabricated. It is intended for use by project technicians who can then advise potters and producers of the best possible mixes. The tests are simple, but we recommend that they are carried out in a laboratory. Basic mathematics is the only skill required to do the calculations and a meticulous approach to 'note-taking' helps to build up a long-term record of clay and its characteristics.

Stoves are ideally suited for manufacture by experienced rural potters or in small factories producing, for example, bricks and tiles. Here, the fabrication practices are likely to be suitable for stoves but the clay body mixes are certain to require some modification. Stoves are subjected to more severe service conditions than bricks and tiles, or even cooking pots.

To ensure good sales, stoves should not fail in use from thermally-induced stresses and they should be sufficiently strong to withstand the mechanical loads and knocks to which they are subjected. To make them durable is likely to require more than the use of a suitable clay body mixture. The design and the shape are also important, as is the care taken in their manufacture. We include in this manual some comments on design and fabrication but as this is a very inadequately researched area we can only offer the most basic suggestions.

A research project was carried out at Sheffield University by A. Gaspe under the supervision of P.F. Messer to investigate why pottery stoves or liners made at some locations failed in service through thermally-induced stresses, while those made at other locations did not. The project was funded by the Overseas Development Administration of the UK Government and administered by ITDG in Rugby, UK. The results are presented in the following chapters.

Finally, for those with some scientific background, we provide some information on the factors determining the strength of ceramic materials and the factors affecting the development of thermally-induced stresses.

1

2. Factors affecting strength and thermally-induced stresses

The strength, σ_f, of a ceramic is the tensile stress (force/unit area) at which the material breaks. It depends on the Young's modulus of elasticity, E, of the ceramic, its effective surface energy for fracture initiation, γi, and the size of the fracture-initiating flaw, c, in the following way:

$$\sigma_f = \text{constant} \times \left(\frac{E\gamma i}{c}\right)^{0.5}$$

The constant depends on the shape, position and orientation of the fracture-initiating flaw.

The product $E\gamma i$ determines the toughness of the ceramic. The fracture toughness, K_{ic}, is given by:

$$K_{ic} = (2E\gamma i)^{0.5}$$

Flaws are regions from which the material is missing and through which mechanical load or force cannot be transmitted. Flaws concentrate the stress around their peripheries. A spherical pore is a flaw but, because of its rounded shape, the maximum stress is only twice the average value as shown in Figure 1. The maximum stress does not change with the size of the spherical pore. Rounded pores, even large ones, are unlikely to be fracture-initiating flaws on their own. To be severe, a flaw needs to be either a sharp crack or a pore linked to a sharp crack. This is because the stress next to the crack tip is magnified by a factor very much greater than two.

Inclusions such as quartz grains are often partially or wholly detached from the matrix by cracks or by associated pores or fissures (a fissure is an elongated pore which concentrates stress by more than a factor of two). Therefore, inclusions often act as quasi-pores (see Figure 3), which can be linked with sharp cracks to become fracture-initiating flaws.

When the mechanical load on a material is increased, the stress within the material is also increased. Adjacent to a flaw, the stress will reach the very high value required to pull the atoms apart, whilst the average stress is at a modest level. When the bonds between the atoms are ruptured, the flaw grows in size at the crack from the flaw tip and propagates across the material causing the material to split into at least two parts.

We know from the examination of fracture surfaces that large pores – both of rounded and elongated shape – and inclusions cause fracture. We know theoretically that these flaws must have had a sharp crack-like feature associated with them to make them severe flaws. The equation for strength tells us that the strength of a ceramic decreases as the flaw size increases.

The terms E and γi in the equation both depend on the effective porosity in the ceramic; that is, on the volume function of pores and quasi-pores. Both E and γi decrease as the effective porosity increases.

For E, this occurs because pores and quasi-

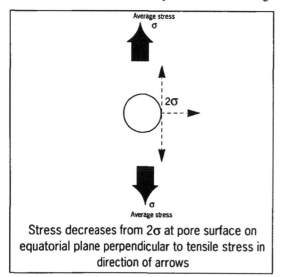

Stress decreases from 2σ at pore surface on equatorial plane perpendicular to tensile stress in direction of arrows

Figure 1: Stress around a spherical pore

pores cannot support and transmit a force. Consequently, the material around the pore or quasi-pore is more highly stressed, as shown in Figure 1. A material is therefore stretched more for a given mechanical load when it is porous than when it is fully dense. A porous material therefore has a lower value of E.

Energy is required to fracture any material. Part of the energy is required to form the new surface. Energy is expended in other ways, such as heating the material. The total energy requirement to form each unit area of fracture surface is γi. During fracture a propagating crack is attracted towards pores and quasi-pores lying close to its path, i.e. it takes the path of least resistance. If it intersects the pores and quasi-pores, less surface has to be created when the material is fractured. Consequently the presence of pores and quasi-pores lowers the value of γi.

For a flaw of fixed size, type, position and orientation, the strength will decrease as the effective porosity is increased (E, γi and K_{ic} decrease).

When an object is heated non-uniformly, the temperature varies with position throughout the object. As materials expand when they are heated, the object expands but by different amounts throughout its volume because of the temperature variation. The part which is at the highest temperature wants to expand the most. Its expansion will be constrained by a neighbouring part which is at a lower temperature and wants, therefore, to expand less. The hotter part is constrained to be smaller than it wants to be, whilst the cooler part is forced to be larger. This is how thermal stresses arise. The hotter part is in compression, whilst the cooler part is in tension.

Thermally-induced stresses depend on the thermal expansion coefficient (TEC), the moduli of elasticity, such as E, and the temperature gradient. The stress will increase when any of these factors is increased.

The presence of pores does not significantly affect the TEC, although, as already discussed, they reduce E and the other elastic moduli.

Quartz particles undergo a contraction on being cooled through 573°C as they transform from the β to the α form. Also, the TEC of α–quartz is high, so that on cooling after the transformation quartz undergoes a large contraction. Quartz particles contract more on cooling than the surrounding pottery matrix and this generates stresses which cause large quartz particles (greater than 40µm diameter) to detach themselves from the matrix to form quasi-pores. Small quartz particles, below 10µm, may not break away. Those that remain attached increase the TEC of the pottery, whilst those that are detached do not affect the TEC below 573°C.

Consequently, thermally-induced stresses can be reduced by increasing the effective porosity.

Thermally-induced stresses may also be reduced by designing the object so that it can easily change its shape on being heated. To illustrate this, consider the cylindrical tube, shown in section in Figure 2a, which is heated internally so that the inner surface is hotter than the outer surface.

The tube will develop a compressive hoop stress around the inner surface and a tensile hoop stress around the outer surface. If the tube is slit along its length to produce a very thin gap of a negligible thickness, as shown in section in Figure 2b, the shape of the tube and the gap will change when the tube is heated internally. If the gap were to be brought back to its original width and shape, by applying forces to the tube, the tube would be stressed as in Figure 2a. When the tube is allowed to change shape (Figure 2c), the thermally-induced stresses will be much reduced in magnitude and, in some cases, will be absent.

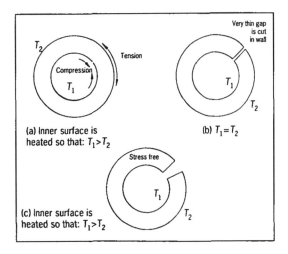

(a) Inner surface is heated so that: $T_1 > T_2$

(b) $T_1 = T_2$

(c) Inner surface is heated so that: $T_1 > T_2$

Figure 2: Ceramic tubes develop stress as shown when heated from inside

3. The tendency of stoves and stove liners to fail from thermally-induced stresses

The research project at Sheffield University investigating why pottery stoves or liners made at some locations failed in service through thermally-induced stresses examined ten clays from various locations throughout Asia and Africa which were being used to make stoves and liners. The tendency of the stoves and liners made from these clays to fail in service from thermally-induced stresses was assessed by Tim Jones of ITDG. He reported their behaviour as varying from very good to very bad. An attempt was made to correlate this observed behaviour with characteristic properties of the clays.

A correlation was found between the clay/non-clay ratio (C/NC ratio) and the tendency of the stoves and liners to fail in service. Each natural clay was considered to be composed of two parts. The material below 2μm was considered to be the clay component and that above 2μm the non-clay component. The C/NC ratio is simply the ratio of the proportions by weight of the two component parts. Stoves and liners made with natural clays with a value for the C/NC ratio of below 1 had good in-service performance, whereas those with a ratio of more than 1 performed badly. The performance worsened as the value of the ratio increased.

The C/NC ratio is a very incomplete description of a natural clay; many different clays would have the same value ratio. In addition, the processing operations used by various stove-making groups are bound to have differed in certain respects. For example, the drying stage may have been carried out with different degrees of care. Consequently, it is very surprising that a correlation was found. This indicates that the proportion of clay in the starting material has a very strong effect on important characteristics of the material while variations in processing, within sensible limits, are less significant.

The question arises as to why the ratio strongly affects the ability of a stove or liner to withstand the thermal stresses met in service. The reasons considered to be important are given in the next section.

4. The effect of the clay/non-clay ratio on stove behaviour

Drying shrinkage and strength after firing

It is well known that drying shrinkage is strongly affected by the C/NC ratio. With a higher proportion of clay mineral in the raw material, it will shrink more during drying. The tendency for splits to occur will increase with greater shrinkage because shrinkage occurs non-uniformly with non-uniform drying. This causes stresses to develop, which can be relieved by the formation of fissures or splits. Either numerous small fissures or fewer, larger fissures may develop. The larger fissures will not heal during firing. Hence, fired stoves or liners made of material with a high value for the C/NC ratio may contain larger fracture-initiating flaws than those made with material having a lower C/NC ratio. The former would exhibit lower fired strength.

This point may be illustrated by comparing some results obtained by Auke Koopman in Sri Lanka with results obtained in Sheffield for the effect of quartz sand additions on the strength of the fired bodies.

In Koopman's work, test-pieces were produced plastically and these shrank on drying. It was found that the strength first increased and then decreased as quartz sand was progressively added.

In Sheffield, test-pieces were made by pressing moist powder and these did not shrink on drying. Starting from material that contained practically no quartz, it was found that the strength decreased as quartz was progressively added. The decrease is considered to result from the quartz grains creating quasi-pores in the fired materials when they break away from the matrix on cooling from the firing temperature (see Figure 3). The consequent decrease in load-bearing area and

fraction surface to be formed would reduce the fracture toughness of the material and, for a fixed flaw size, decrease the strength.

The initial increase in strength observed in the Dutch work must, therefore, be explained by a reduction in the size of the fracture-initiating flaws as quartz was first added. This could have arisen from the expected reduction in drying shrinkage with increased quartz content.

Effective porosity, strength and thermally-induced stresses

As the C/NC ratio decreases, the effective porosity will increase because of the quasi-pores associated with quartz grains and other inclusions.

As already discussed, the fracture toughness and the thermally-induced stresses will be affected by a change in effective porosity. Although fracture toughness will decrease as the C/NC ratio decreases, the strength of plastically-formed objects may increase. An increase in strength coupled with the reduction in the

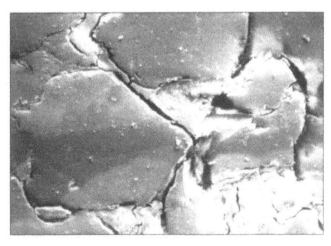

Figure 3: Scanning electron micrograph showing resulting cracks in quasi-pore formation, around a quartz particle

magnitude of the thermally-induced stress that will accompany a decrease in the C/NC ratio should make stoves made with low values of the ratio more able to withstand the service conditions.

The anisotropy of shrinkage and residual stress development

It is well known that when clay-containing bodies are formed plastically, the clay particles become aligned. Clay minerals have particles which are plate-like in shape. During plastic forming, the material is sheared. Slip occurs in slip bands, consisting of clay particles and water. In these, the clay platelets line up with their large plane faces parallel so that they can easily slip over one another. Between the slip bands, the more isometric quartz and feldspar particles form a band in which little or no deformation occurs. These regions also contain clay and water, but the clay particles are arranged between and around the coarser particles and are not preferentially aligned with the slip bands. This is illustrated in Figure 4. Fewer slip bands and/or narrower slip bands should be formed as the concentration of clay in the mixture is reduced and the material becomes less workable.

When a plastically-formed body dries, the shrinkage that occurs is anisotropic. That is, it varies with direction such that shrinkage in the direction perpendicular to slip bands is greater than that parallel to the slip bands. The reason for this is readily explained: there are more water films between clay particles in the direction perpendicular to the slip bands than in the parallel direction.

When plastically-formed bodies are fired, the shrinkage is again anisotropic. This is illustrated in the graphs shown in Figure 5. One reason for anisotropic firing shrinkage is that there is a different number of spaces between clay particles in directions perpendicular and parallel to the slip bands. Another reason is that the dehydroxylation of the clay particles causes them individually to shrink anisotropically.

If a sheet of plastic clay body is produced by rolling or extrusion, the clay platelets are preferentially aligned such that their large plane faces are parallel to the large plane surfaces of the sheet. Drying and firing shrinkages will be greater through the thickness of the sheet. However, this anisotropic shrinkage can occur without macroscopic stresses developing in the sheet. This is because the shrinkage through the thickness does not affect shrinkage in perpendicular directions and vice versa.

Consider a tube produced from a plastic body by extrusion or jollying. The large plane surfaces of the clay particles are now aligned tangentially to the cylindrical surfaces in which they lie within the tube (Figure 6). The radial shrinkage of the tube during drying and firing should be greater than the circumferential shrinkage. However, in this case, shrinkage in a radial direction cannot occur without causing circumferential shrinkage and vice versa. It is easy to deduce that shrinkage in this case leads to the development of stress, such that there is a

Non-clay fragments such as quartz and feldspar

Slip band composed of clay platelets and water

Figure 4: Formation of slip band in a plastic body containing clay and non-clay materials, as a result of shearing

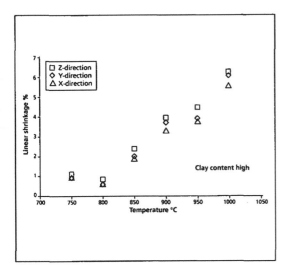 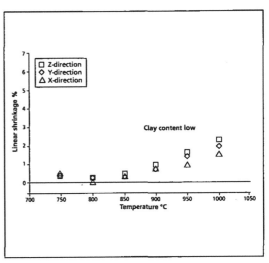

Figure 5: Directional linear shrinkages of plastically-formed test-pieces, produced by rolling natural clay

Note: X *is the direction of rolling*
Y *is perpendicular to the rolling direction, but parallel to the rolled surface of the test-piece*
Z *is perpendicular to both the X and Y directions (most shrinkage occurs in this direction)*

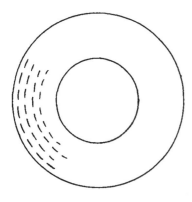

Figure 6: Cross-section of a ceramic tube showing (enlarged) clay particles tangentially aligned to the cylindrical surface

circumferential tensile hoop stress around the outer surface of the tube and a compressive hoop stress around the inner surface. The presence of the stresses affects the shrinkage that occurs.

Stresses may be partially relieved by distortion of the ceramic article during drying or firing and by developing fissures that may subsequently act as fracture-initiating flaws.

Therefore, the consequences of any large-scale, non-planar arrangement of the clay platelets in a stove will be detrimental to its ability to resist thermally-induced stresses, either because of flaws that have formed or because of the residual stress.

For these reasons, stoves or liners made from natural clays with higher C/NC ratio values are likely to be more highly stressed in tension on their outer surfaces. On heating up during cooking, these outer surfaces will be further stressed in tension. When the combined stresses reach the level of the fracture strength, failure occurs.

The presence of residual stress has been demonstrated by extruding small cylindrical tubes. After firing, these were cut along their lengths and found to spring open. Measurements of the strain after cutting have been made so that estimates of the residual stresses could be obtained. This was done for tubes having a range of clay/quartz ratios. It was found that the residual stresses decreased as the ratio decreased. This would be expected as the anisotropy of shrinkage and the overall shrinkage will be reduced as the proportion of clay is reduced. Residual stresses were estimated for tubes made with a high C/NC ratio to be a sizeable fraction of their tensile strength.

The residual stresses that develop in a stove or liner are too complex to be evaluated or even envisaged as there are many changes in the alignment throughout the structure.

5. Avoidance of thermally-induced stress failure

Stoves will fail in service when thermally-induced stress adds to any residual stress present to exceed the fracture strength. The general principle behind improving the serviceable life of a ceramic stove is therefore to minimize both the residual stress and the thermal stress while trying to maintain the fracture strength. To achieve this, there are a number of actions that can be taken.

1. The C/NC ratio should have a value that is not greater than 1. When the ratio is higher than 1, it should be lowered by making additions of a non-clay compound, such as sand. Lowering the C/NC ratio brings benefits resulting from the reduction of shrinkage and the anisotropy of shrinkage during drying and firing. However, if quartz is added, it reduces the fracture-toughness which means the material will be more readily chipped by mechanical impacts. For the manufacture of all ceramic stoves, a value for the ratio which is below but close to 1 will generally be required, whereas a lower value of about 0.6 would be suitable for a stove liner that does not need to be as mechanically robust.

2. Residual stresses and thermally-induced stress can be reduced by making appropriately placed cuts in the stoves. For a single-pot stove, a single vertical cut would suffice. For a two-pot stove with interconnecting chimney, ideally a cut is required in each section. However, excellent results have been obtained with a single cut in the firing chamber. A possible position for the cut is shown in Figure 7.

A problem arises when cuts are made in unfired stoves. An offset has been found to develop in the firing chamber of the stove as it dries and is fired. This can prevent the pot forming an adequate seal with the firing chamber. The reason for the occurrence of the asymmetric distortion is not understood. However, it has been found by Sulpya-Recast, Nepal, that the offset can be prevented by wrapping a strip of pottery body completely around the cut section to stop any differential movement. The strip is placed in position when the stove is sufficiently dry to avoid the strip bonding to the stove. After firing, the strip is carefully broken to remove it.

3. Select a clay preparation process and a means of forming the clay that causes the minimum amount of

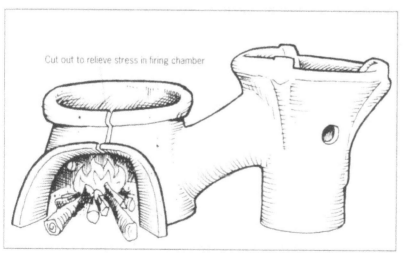

Cut out to relieve stress in firing chamber

Figure 7: A ceramic stove from Sri Lanka with a stress-relieving cut in the combustion chamber

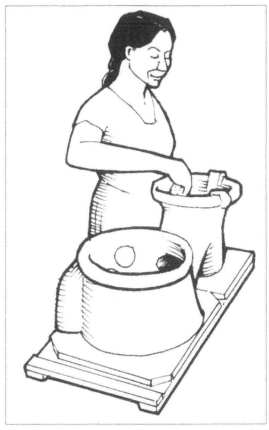

Figure 8: Flat pallets help stoves to dry uniformly and stress free

4. Dry stoves slowly and evenly on flat pallets (Figure 8) and under polythene in hot and draughty conditions. Remember that during drying, residual stresses often form as a result of anisotropic shrinkage and that flaws can appear, especially if the drying is uneven.

5. Do not over-fire the ceramic. This will tend to lower the true porosity and would require a greater proportion of non-clay, i.e. quasi-pores, to help compensate for the loss of true porosity.

6. Make sure the clay is a homogenous mix if different clays have been used and check that small stones and debris have been removed so that points likely to concentrate the stress are minimized.

7. Very little is known about the effects of stove design, shape and configuration on the overall durability, and at this stage it is best to keep stove designs simple. Avoid sharp corners and tight bends and reinforce areas such as doorways and passages (Figure 9). When joining parts, use clays of equal moisture, score the joints lightly, use a well-prepared slip and apply firm pressure without over-deforming the parts.

particle alignment. Experiences indicate that hand coiling is better than throwing which in turn is better than jigger jollying. Experiences also indicate that changing the production process is not easy, in which case the C/NC ratio may have to be adjusted to compensate. As a general rule, the greater the particle alignment that will result from a certain production process the more non-clay should be added. However, there will be limits as to how much non-clay can be added before the clay body loses its plasticity and/or workability.

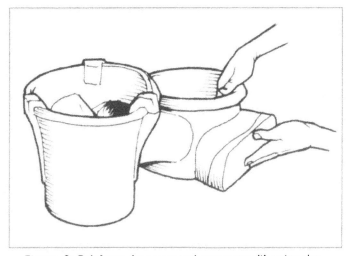

Figure 9: Reinforce doorways and passages with extra clay

6. Selection and preparation of clay bodies for stove manufacture

Naturally-occurring clays are extremely complex materials. They are composed of a variety of minerals, which can be divided into clay minerals and non-clay minerals.

Disordered kaolinite, illite, montmorillonite, chlorite, mixed-layer clay minerals and, to a lesser extent, well-ordered kaolinite are the clay minerals found in natural clays.

The most common non-clay minerals are: quartz, feldspar, carbonates and iron minerals. Some of them would act as fluxes during the sintering process if the temperature were to reach a sufficiently high value, i.e. they could promote densification by causing liquid formation. However, in most stove and liner production, the firing temperature will not be high enough for a liquid phase to form.

Experience has shown that certain clays and non-clays are not suitable for inclusion in stove clay bodies. For example, montmorillonite is an extremely fine clay and gives exceptional plasticity. However, it also has an exceptionally high shrinkage, which means on drying and firing it is likely to develop high residual stress and numerous fissures. It is therefore extremely weak after firing. The greater the proportion of montmorillonite in a raw clay the weaker it is likely to be. For clays that have very high amounts of montmorillonite, no amount of adjusting the C/NC ratio is likely to improve their strength. Therefore clays that contain montmorillonite are unlikely to be good clays for stoves. Detecting the presence of montmorillonite is difficult and can only be done in a well-equipped laboratory. However, as a simple guide, very high shrinkage rates will be an indication of montmorillonite.

Another common problem with raw clay is the presence of carbonates in the form of limestone which can lead to lime blowing. The presence of limestone can also affect the accuracy of the C/NC ratio and therefore when clays are being tested the limestone is best removed with hydrochloric acid (see Test procedure on page 12). Clays that contain very high levels of carbonates and/or exhibit lime blowing are best abandoned.

Determination of clay/non-clay ratio in natural clay body

The determination of mineral phases present in a natural clay can be done using X-ray diffraction. However, the work at Sheffield University shows that the proportions of minerals that exist in the clay are more important than the actual mineral. Determining this has proved to be impossible or very complicated because of the following:

1. the unavailability of reference samples required for calibration;
2. the unavoidable tendency for the particles of clay minerals to become aligned during sample preparation, which affects the X-ray diffraction pattern.

To overcome this, a simple technique was developed to measure the amount of the clay mineral in a natural clay so that the C/NC ratio can be calculated.

All clay minerals show characteristic weight losses because they undergo dehydroxylation when heated in the temperature range of 400°C – 700°C. The dehydroxylation weight loss for a given mixture of clay minerals should be constant and is a function of the amount of the individual clays present and their characteristic weight losses. This weight loss is the basis of the method to determine the C/NC ratio.

The method involves the following few stages:

1. separation of the clay fraction – i.e. the sub 2μm fraction;
2. heat treatment of samples of the raw clay and the separated fraction to remove organic

impurities, which would otherwise interfere with the characteristic weight losses;

3. measurement of the dehydroxylation weight losses for the raw clay and the separated fraction;

4. calculation of the weight loss ratio which gives the clay mineral content.

Theoretical background on separation of the clay fraction below 2μm

Sedimentation can be used to separate the size fraction below 2μm from the coarse particles, which are the non-clay minerals. The method is based on Stoke's law of settling for individual spherical particles falling freely at a steady velocity under the influence of gravity, resisted only by the viscous drag of the medium.

For a particle of diameter d in a dilute suspension, the steady or terminal velocity v is given by:

$$v = d^2 \frac{\rho_S - \rho_L}{18\eta} \cdot g \qquad (1)$$

where ρ_S is the density of the particle, ρ_L is the density of the suspending liquid, g is the acceleration due to gravity and η is the viscosity of the suspending liquid.

The time, t, taken for a spherical particle moving at the terminal velocity to fall through a height, h, is given by:

$$t = \frac{h}{v} \qquad (2)$$

Substitution for v from equation 2 in equation 1 gives:

$$t = \frac{18\eta}{d^2 (\rho_S - \rho_L) g} h \qquad (3)$$

Using equation 3, the time can be calculated for 2μm particle to settle through a given height.

Example calculation

$$d = 2\mu m = 2 \times 10^4 \, cm$$

$$\rho_S = 2.6g \, cm^{-3}$$

(Typical value for density of clay)

$$\rho_L = 1.0g \, cm^{-3}$$

(It can be assumed that the density of the suspending liquid is similar to water, since Stoke's law can only be applied for the dilute suspensions)

$$\eta = 0.0079 g \, cm^{-1} s^{-1}$$

(This is the value for the viscosity of water at 30°C: the viscosity of water changes significantly with temperature as can be seen from Table 1.)

$$g = 981 cm \, s^{-2}$$

Substituting these values in equation 3:

$$t = \frac{18 \times 0.0079 g \, cm^{-1} s^{-1} h}{4 \times 10^{-8} cm^2 (2.6 - 1.0) g \, cm^{-3} \times 981 cm \, s^{-2}}$$

$$= (2264.9) h \, cm^{-1} s$$

If $h = 10$ (i.e. the 2μm particle settles through a height of 10cm under the above conditions)

$$t = 22649 \text{ seconds}$$

This means a particle of 2μm will take 6 hours and 17 minutes to fall 10cm in a dilute suspension at 30°C.

Table 2 show the times for 2μm particles to settle through various heights at different temperatures.

Table 1: Effect of temperature on the viscosity of water

Temperature (°C)	Viscosity (cm s⁻¹)
16	0.0111
18	0.0105
20	0.0100
22	0.0095
24	0.0091
26	0.0087
28	0.0083
30	0.0079
32	0.0076
34	0.0073
36	0.0070
38	0.0068
40	0.0065
42	0.0063
44	0.0061
46	0.0058

Table 2: The times taken for 2μm particles to settle through various heights at different temperatures

Height (cm)	Temperature (°C)	Settling time (h:min)
10	25	7:05
	30	6:17
	35	5:42
	40	5:11
15	25	10:38
	30	9:26
	35	8:32
	40	7:46
20	25	14:11
	30	12:35
	35	11:23
	40	10:21
30	25	21:16
	30	18:52
	35	17:05
	40	15:32

Test procedure

The test procedure to determine the C/NC ratio of a natural clay body is given below.

1. Select a representative sample of dried clay, about 1kg.

2. Crush the clay with something like a mortar and pestle to produce a powder with agglomerates no bigger than 1mm.

3. Select a bucket with a volume of about 9 litres (35cm in height, 25cm diameter at the top).

4. 3cm from the top of the bucket, make a mark and 10cm below this, make a second mark.

5. Add water to the bucket to fill about half the volume. Then add 800g of dried clay and 8g of Calgon (calcium chloride) as a deflocculant and soak overnight.

6. Stir thoroughly, preferably with a mechanical stirrer.

7. Add water to bring suspension up to the top mark on the bucket and stir to homogenize suspension. (This will make a suspension containing about 10% solids.)

8. Measure the temperature of the suspension.

9. Leave, for the time calculated for this temperature, the 2μm particles of clay to settle through a height of 10cm. Use equation 3 or use Table 2.

10. Syphon off the suspension to the lower (10cm) mark on the bucket, being careful not to remove any suspension below this depth.

11. Add more water to the bucket, raising the level to the top mark on the bucket. Mix the suspension thoroughly and repeat the sedimentation process, i.e. follow steps 9 and 10.

12. Add the two syphoned-off suspensions together.

13. The water can be removed from the suspension of the sub 2μm fraction by boiling in a metal pan. To avoid the dehydroxylation at this stage (400°C – 700°C), remove from the heat whilst some water remains. Alternatively, the suspensions may be centrifuged to remove the bulk of water.

14. If carbonates have been found in the clay, by testing a sample of the raw clay with dilute hydrochloric acid (HCl), the carbon dioxide (CO_2) must be removed before determining the dehydroxylation weight losses. If no carbonates have been detected, proceed to step 15.

Note. It is possible that most of the carbonate particles will have been removed from the sub 2μm fraction by sedimentation, so that this material may not exhibit a significant weight loss of CO_2 when it is heated to 700°C. However, this assumption can be tested by treating a small sample of dry, sedimented clay with dilute HCl. If carbonates are not found to be present, carry out the procedure given in step 15. If carbonates are still present, dilute HCl should be added to the sub 2μm fraction to produce a thin paste. This can be done in the crucible to be used for heating the clay to remove the organic material. The dilute acid remaining after reaction with the carbonates will be removed during this heat treatment.

The raw clay sample containing carbonates has to be treated with acid. As more and coarser particles of the carbonates will be present in the raw clay, more thorough acid treatment is required for their removal. About 200g of dried, ground clay should be placed in the crucible to be used for the heat-treatment to remove the organic material. Dilute HCl should be stirred occasionally with an implement that does not react with the acid. This could be made of glass, plastic or wood. When bubbles cease to form, more acid should be added and the slurry stirred. This process should be repeated until no bubbles form after an addition of acid.

The slurry should be left to sediment and the clear liquid layer that forms carefully poured off without removing any particles. The more concentrated slurry can be dried during the heat treatment to remove organic material.

15. The organic material can be removed from the raw clay and clay fraction by heating to 375°C and soaking for 8 hours. All the clay fraction after drying should be placed in a crucible and given this heat treatment. About 200g of raw clay should be similarly heat treated in another crucible.

16. To determine the dehydroxylation weight losses from the raw clay and the clay fraction, known weights of the two materials after removal of the organic material, should be heated in crucibles to 700°C for 3 hours. All of the raw clay sample and clay fraction heat treated at 375°C should be used.

The weights of the raw clay sample and clay fraction after dehydroxylation must be determined and subtracted from the initial weights of these samples, to determine the weight losses. All weights should be determined to ±0.1g or better.

17. The amount of clay mineral in the raw clay can be estimated by calculating the ratio of dehydroxylation weight loss of the raw clay to that of the sub 2µm fraction. If the amount of clay present is known, the C/NC ratio can be easily determined.

Example calculation

Weight of the raw clay after heat treatment at 375°C = W_1

Weight of the clay fraction after heat treatment at 375°C = W_2

Weight of the raw clay after heat treatment at 700°C = W_3

Weight of the clay fraction after heat treatment at 700°C = W_4
Dehydroxylation weight loss of raw clay = $(W_1 - W_3)$

Dehydroxylation weight loss of clay fraction = $(W_2 - W_4)$

Clay mineral content of raw clay (natural clay body)

$$= \frac{(W_1 - W_3)}{(W_2 - W_4)} \times 100 = x\%$$

Therefore non-clay mineral content = $(100 - x)\%$

$$C / NC \text{ ratio} = \frac{x}{(100 - x)}$$

Adjustment of clay body

Natural clays containing more clay materials than non-clay materials, i.e. with a ratio greater than 1, can be adjusted to be suitable for stove fabrication. This can be achieved by adding a predetermined amount of a non-clay material such as fine quartz (possibly paddy husk ash) or fine feldspar sand to reduce the ratio.

This can be done by measuring the weight of the raw clay sample before and after drying at about 110°C overnight.

Assume that the weight of a wet sample of

raw clay is $W_w$kg. After drying, let the weight be $W_d$kg. Let the initial C/NC ratio be R_i and the required final value R_f, where R_i is greater than R_f. Then let the weight of non-clay material to be added to the clay sample be $W_a$kg. The relationship between these variables can be represented by:

$$W_a = \frac{W_d(R_i - R_f)}{R_f(1 + R_i)}$$

The non-clay mineral can be added to the wet clay, so that $W_a$kg of the non-clay mineral is added to every $W_d$kg of wet clay provided that water content is constant. Alternatively, $W_a$kg of non-clay mineral should be added to every $W_d$kg of dry clay.

Numerical example

One kilo of wet raw clay is found to contain 0.2kg of water (i.e. 0.8kg of dry raw clay). The raw clay has a C/NC ratio of 1.5. A final ratio of 0.9 is required. What weight of non-clay mineral should be added?

i.e.

$$W_w = 1\text{kg} \qquad W_d = 0.8\text{kg}$$
$$R_i = 1.5 \qquad R_f = 0.9$$

therefore

$$W_a = \frac{0.8(1.5 - 0.9)}{0.9(1 + 1.5)}$$

$$= \frac{0.8 \times 0.6}{0.9 \times 2.5} = 0.213\text{kg}$$

Therefore, for every kilo of wet clay, add 0.21kg of non-clay mineral or to every 0.8kg of dry clay, add 0.21kg of non-clay mineral, i.e. for every kilo of dry clay, add 0.27kg of non-clay mineral.

7. Testing the effects of adjusting the clay/non-clay ratio

It has been stated earlier that the C/NC ratio should be around 1, i.e. equal parts of clay (2µm in size and below) and non-clay (particles larger than 2µm). However, for many clays this is likely to vary because choosing the correct C/NC ratio can also depend on the fired hardness and method of manufacture.

In many projects it therefore becomes necessary to check before launching the stove in the market place that adjustments to the clay have actually resulted in an improvement and by how much.

This can be checked very approximately by carrying out destructive testing either in the laboratory using controlled conditions or in the field under actual use conditions.

A number of projects in Sri Lanka, Kenya and Nepal have conducted destructive testing in the laboratory using the following method. Samples of stoves are made with clays with various C/NC ratios. For example, two samples such as a raw clay and the same clay adjusted to a C/NC ratio with 1. The stoves are repeatedly fired with wood or charcoal and cooled until they crack. The number of heating cycles endured by the stoves will indicate the clay's durability.

There are a number of problems associated with this approach. The heating and cooling cycles must be severe in order to crack the stove within a reasonably short time, otherwise the tests may go on for many days. Firing and cooling the stoves in exactly the same way for each of the samples and for each test is difficult. There are likely to be manufacturing flaws in the stoves which can cause cracking. To ensure the results of such destructive testing are accurate it is important to test as large a sample size as possible. Because this can often be an expensive process it is advised that the sample size is at least five. If the results are scattered then the sample size can be increased.

A more realistic way of checking the effects of changes to the clay body is to monitor the lifetimes of samples of stoves under actual use conditions.

Stoves are made with various C/NC ratios and they are distributed to households for use. A system needs to be arranged so that the stoves can be checked periodically for cracking. Lifetimes can be expressed as numbers of meals cooked, or in days or weeks. Like laboratory tests, field tests have inaccuracies. In addition, the use conditions are even less controlled and the sample size should be as large as possible. Because there is likely to be less physical work involved compared to laboratory tests, the sample size can be much larger. It is advised that this should not be less than 20 for each clay recipe.

It takes a long time to perfect a good clay body and the required effort and costs should not be underestimated. Planning and meticulous note-taking are the essential elements to developing good recipes.

Before a good clay recipe is discovered many series of tests may be necessary. For only one type of clay it could easily take three series of tests to arrive at a good recipe. For example:

1st series –	Raw clay versus raw clay adjusted to C/NC ratio of 1.
2nd series –	C/NC ratio less than 1 versus C/NC ratio greater than 1.
3rd series –	Final recipe.

To do even one series of tests can easily take two to three months.

Clay testing –	2 weeks
Preparation of clays to make stoves –	1 week
Construction of stoves –	2 weeks

Drying and firing –	3 weeks
Destructive testing –	2 weeks

(minimum, and may be as long as 6 months)

Many projects seriously underestimate the time required to carry out clay testing, mostly because potters are not always available to make stoves when needed. The construction process can take a long time due to the drying process. There is often a temptation to rush this phase and consequently manufacturing errors can occur which can cause cracking either in the firing or early on in use. This will seriously affect the destructive testing results.

Appendix

Equipment and facilities

The following equipment is required and is likely to be found in most science laboratories. If possible the tests should be carried out also in the laboratory since it will then be easier to maintain accuracy.

- Mortar and pestle to crush 1kg of clay.

- A 10-litre bucket of height 35cm and diameter 25cm (approximate dimensions). Remember that if several clays are to be tested at the same time it will be useful to have several buckets.

- Calgon (calcium chloride) as a deflocculant.

- A wooden paddle or mechanical stirrer.

- Stop-watch to time the settling process.

- Thermometer to measure the temperature of the suspension.

- Short length of hosepipe to syphon off suspension.

- A stove and metal vessel to boil off water from suspension, or a centrifuge.

- Hydrochloric acid and small vessel to check whether raw clay contains carbonates.

- Small kiln (preferably electric) with temperature control to fire clay samples up to 700°C for 3 hours. Wood-fired kilns may be used for this operation providing the temperatures can be held for the durations specified. The size of kiln will depend on the size of crucibles and numbers used per firing. In most cases 2 cubic feet of firing chamber is likely to be adequate.

- Crucibles or beakers capable of withstanding up to 700°C for 3 hours without any loss in weight. They must be sufficiently large to hold 200g of clay powder. Remember that if several clays are to be fired at the same time it will be useful to have several crucibles. Each crucible can be used only once. If these cannot be purchased, local potters can make them from a good pottery clay (fire them well at over 750°C for 3 hours, otherwise they may lose weight during the test firing).

- Weighing machine or balance accurate to 0.1g.

Milton Keynes UK
Ingram Content Group UK Ltd.
UKHW011338070824
1191UKWH00034B/253